Presented To

A JEWISH BESTIARY

*Our Rabbis said: Even those things which you may regard
as completely superfluous to the creation of the world, such
as fleas, gnats, and flies, even they too are included in the
creation of the world, and the Holy One, blessed be He, car-
ries out His purpose through everything, even through a
snake, a scorpion, a gnat, or a frog.*

Genesis Rabbah

A JEWISH BESTIARY

A Book of Fabulous Creatures Drawn

from Hebraic Legend and Lore by

MARK PODWAL

The Jewish Publication Society of America • Philadelphia • 1984 • 5744

Library of Congress Cataloging in Publication Data

Podwal, Mark H., 1945-
   A Jewish bestiary.

   Bibliography: p.
      1. Animals in art.   2. Animals, Mythical, in art.
I. Title.
NC139.P59A4   1984   704.9'46   84-14421
ISBN 0-8276-0245-6

Designed by Adrianne Onderdonk Dudden

For Ayalah

CONTENTS

PREFACE   The world of the animal kingdom is deeply ingrained in the Jewish consciousness, no doubt prompted by the majestic account of Creation: "God said, 'Let the waters bring forth swarms of living creatures, and birds that fly above the earth across the expanse of the sky. . . . Let the earth bring forth every kind of living creature: cattle, creeping things, and wild beasts of every kind.' " Indeed, a "Jewish bestiary" might very well start with the Hebrew Bible, which abounds in animal references—the serpent of the Garden of Eden, the beasts and birds that join Noah in the ark, Balaam's talking ass, the red heifer, the lion of Judah, the leopard that lies down with the kid (in Isaiah's noble prophesy), the awesome creatures of land and sea depicted in the Book of Job, the insect that instructs the sluggard, to cite but a few. Seven of the twelve tribes of Israel are represented by animal symbols.

Moreover, there is a rich store of animal tales to be found in talmudic and midrashic literature, where the creatures in question convey a variety of moral lessons. (For example, according to the Midrash, only after Moses had shown kindness to a lamb did God entrust him with leading his human flock, Israel.) Jewish legend and folklore also play host to an assortment of fantastic creatures, such as the *ziz*, the *shamir*, and the *tahash*, which, like some of the more readily observed denizens of the animal world, were called into being to carry out certain divinely ordained tasks.

These are the animals, real and imaginary, that have stirred my own artistic impulse. From among the vast assemblage, I have chosen to depict twenty-five creatures, culled from traditional Jewish sources, as set forth in the texts that accompany the individual illustrations. They include birds, fish, cattle, creeping things, and wild beasts—all drawn from the wide and wonderful variety of "living creatures" that exert a special force on the Jewish fancy.

Animal representation has long figured in the history of the Jewish book. Indeed, the earliest printed Jewish book containing illustrations, as far as is known, is a collection of medieval animal fables, *Meshal Ha-Kadmoni* ("The Ancient Parable"). Printed in 1491 by the famous Italian-Jewish house of Soncino in Brescia, it contains more than eighty woodcuts (many of animal scenes) copied from the illuminations of Isaac ben Sahula some two centuries before. Altogether, medieval Jewish literature includes several compendiums of animal tales, such as *The Alphabet of Ben Sira* and *Mishlei Shu'alim* ("Fox Fables"). These works, however, cannot be said to belong to the genre of the bestiary, in which creatures, both actual and fabulous, are systematically (often allegorically) portrayed. The Jewish works more closely resemble collections of Aesop-like fables than pictorial treatises on beasts and their habits, that is, bestiaries.

By the thirteenth and fourteenth centuries, the bestiary had achieved a popularity in the Christian world second only to that of the Bible. Derived from Egyptian, Greek, Judaic, and Indian sources, the first bestiary was probably composed in Alexandria in the second century. Attributed to a legendary authority, Physiologus ("the naturalist"), the work itself eventually became known by the same name. The earliest extant illustrated bestiary dates from the ninth century. Medieval bestiaries were almost always accompanied by illustrations, and this combination of text and picture provides the genre with its special charm. Copies of bestiary illustrations, reflecting many misconceptions regarding the natural order, were incorporated into countless medieval manuscripts, and their influence may be seen in church frescoes and façades throughout Europe.

Pictures of beasts appeared frequently in Jewish illuminated manuscripts as well. There were the familiar creatures mentioned in the Bible, most notably the lion, and also exotic creatures, included for decorative purposes. Thus, a giraffe would be depicted because it was strange in appearance and rare among European animals, not because it had any symbolic significance. In addition, there was a host of bizarre hybrids, including cat-dragons, birds with human heads, and lion-eagles. Although sometimes the illustrations of the exotic animals were accurate, more often they were not. Camels frequently resembled horses, and it was not unusual for the humps to be omitted. (Many of the beasts were known to the Jewish illustrators only through the pictures in bestiaries.) There was an even greater variation in the representation of mythological creatures. For instance, in a medieval Spanish-Jewish manuscript the unicorn (associated by some authorities with the biblical *tahash*) resembled a giraffe, whereas in an Italian manuscript it had the body of a horse, cloven rear hoofs, and lion's paws in front.

In addition to being a kind of encyclopedia of the animal kingdom, the bestiary also served as a book of Christian moral and religious instruction. Virtues such as abstinence and chastity were taught through the presentation of animals symbolizing the particular quality. For instance, the phoenix, the bird that rises from its own ashes (derived from Egyptian myth), became for Christians a symbol of the Resurrection. The phoenix also appears in Jewish tradition, but here the bird's immortality is viewed as its reward for refusing to taste the forbidden fruit offered by Eve to all the creatures in Paradise. Nevertheless, the illuminations in Jewish manuscripts do not differ essentially from those in Christian bestiaries, from which they were often copied (a cultural phenomenon that, for better or worse, affords many examples down through the ages). As for the phoenix itself in Jewish tradition, it derives from the apocryphal Book of Enoch, where the bird is described as purple in color with the head of a crocodile, the feet and tail of a lion, and twelve wings. However, in Jewish medieval manuscripts and printed books, the phoenix usually appears simply as a bird on a flaming pyre, similar to the Christian portrayal.

In the drawings that follow I have eschewed such cultural "borrowings," even if there is historical sanction for the practice. What I have sought to create here are bestiary illustrations within a strictly Jewish context. Creatures whose forms are known in nature are pictured according to an attribute ascribed to them in Jewish legend or in relation to tales in which they appear. Thus, a spider plays on King David's harp. The "pious" stork is depicted donning phylacteries. The despised swine is represented merely as a shadow. The fabulous ziz, the greatest of birds and which few have observed, is here depicted only by one of its feathers, which has fluttered to earth.

The collection also includes, as any Jewish bestiary must, creatures first encountered in the Scriptures (and which are also the subjects of Jewish legend and lore)—the dove and the raven of Noah's ark, the sacrificial ram that substituted for Isaac on the altar, the golden calf, the Azazel-goat, and Jonah's great fish, among others. Behemoth—whose description in the Book of Job indicates a real creature, in all likelihood the hippopotamus—here appears in a mythical guise, as does Leviathan, the other great natural wonder cited in the Book of Job.

These creatures have illumined the Jewish imagination throughout the centuries. I hope that their renewed incarnation in these pages may perpetuate their ancient enchantment.

A JEWISH BESTIARY

THE ANT   The Book of Proverbs describes the ant as one of the four creatures that are "among the tiniest on earth, yet they are the wisest of the wise." An exemplary insect ("go to the ant, thou sluggard"), symbol *par excellence* of diligence and foresightedness, the ant prepares for the lean months of winter by gathering stores during the summer.

According to legend, King Solomon and 40,000 of his soldiers once strayed into the valley of the ants. Now Solomon, among his other accomplishments, could converse with all the creatures of the earth, each in its own language. Thus he overheard one ant exhorting its fellows to withdraw, in order to avoid being trampled by the royal army. Solomon ordered his men to halt and summoned the ant that had spoken.

The Queen Ant came forth, and Solomon asked her, "Is there anyone greater than I in all the world?" But she refused to answer unless the king agreed to place her on his hand, hold her up, and speak to her face to face. Solomon acceded and repeated his question: "Is there anyone greater than I in all the world?"

"Yes!" replied the Queen Ant.

"Who?" asked King Solomon.

"I am," said the ant.

"How is that possible?" Solomon raged.

The Queen Ant retorted, "Were I not greater than you, you would not have complied with my demand."

Solomon threw her to the ground, shouting, "Don't you know who I am? I am Solomon, King of Israel, son of King David!"

Whereupon the Queen Ant admonished King Solomon to humility by reminding him that a tiny creature had preceded man in the order of creation. The proud and mighty king, we may presume, was properly chastened.

נמלה

THE SERPENT Of all the animals in Paradise, the serpent was truly the most remarkable. According to legend, only the serpent spoke Hebrew, whereas the rest of the animals conversed in their own special tongues. Resembling man in many ways, the serpent stood erect on two feet. His height was equal to that of the camel. Had it not been for the fall of Adam and Eve, one pair of serpents, it was said, would have been able to perform all of man's labors on earth. Furthermore, the serpent would have supplied earth's inhabitants with gold, silver, and precious stones, for he knew the hiding places of many great treasures.

But the happy role ordained for the serpent was not to be. Envious of the joy that the first man shared with his mate, the serpent plotted to bring about Adam's death so that he could have Eve for himself.

When God sat in judgment on the serpent's actions, He refused to hear the reptile's defense. For the Holy One, blessed be He, knew that the serpent was a crafty debater and would undoubtedly seek to shift the blame to Satan and *his* provocations. After the sentence of doom was pronounced upon the serpent, seventy-one angels descended from Heaven and chopped off his hands and feet and split his tongue. His suffering was so great that his agonized cries could be heard from one end of the earth to the other. Thenceforth he had to crawl on his belly. Among his other punishments, it was decreed that the serpent would vanish from the Holy Land when all Israel walks in the ways of the Lord.

נחש

THE RAM   Abraham, we read in the Bible, was commanded by God to offer up his beloved son Isaac as a sacrifice. The patriarch, obedient to the divine command, took Isaac to Mount Moriah, site of the future Temple, and bound him upon an altar. However, at the crucial moment, an angel of the Lord intervened and a ram, providentially appearing on the scene, served as the offering in Isaac's stead.

Jewish legend relates that the ram, looking to fulfill its destiny, had been running toward Abraham when Satan attempted to seize it; in the process its horns became entangled in a thicket. The Midrash notes: "The Holy One, blessed be He, showed Abraham the ram tearing himself free from one thicket and becoming entangled in another. Said the Holy One, blessed be He, to Abraham: 'Thus are your children destined to be caught in iniquities and entangled in misfortunes, but in the end they will be redeemed by the horns of a ram.' " Another interpretation: Just as the ram extricated itself from one thicket only to be caught in another, so Abraham's children would pass from kingdom to kingdom. Delivered from Babylonia, they would be enslaved by Media; rescued from Media, they would be enslaved by Greece; freed from Greece, they would serve Rome. Yet in the end they would be redeemed by the sound of a ram's horn.

This ram was indeed a special creature. According to legend, it was created during the twilight of the first Sabbath eve and from that time on resided in Paradise, awaiting its moment to take Isaac's place on the altar. All the parts of its carcass were put to extraordinary use. The ashes of the portions burnt on the altar formed the foundation of the inner altar of the Temple. On this altar the sacrifice of atonement was brought once a year on Yom Kippur, the anniversary of the binding of Isaac. From the ram's sinews David made ten strings for his harp. From the wool Elijah fashioned his coat. As for the two horns, the left one was sounded after the Revelation on Mount Sinai. The other will be used to proclaim the advent of the Messiah.

THE LION   Crowned "the king of beasts" by the Talmud, the lion is the emblem of strength, bravery, and majesty. The Hebrew Bible contains more than a hundred references to this royal beast, many of them metaphorical. Comparisons include the tribe of Judah, King David, Israel, the Temple, and even God Himself. "Like as a lion . . . so will the Lord of Hosts come down to fight on Mount Zion," says the prophet Isaiah.

A folk tale recalls a certain fabulous lion.

Once the Roman emperor summoned Rabbi Joshua ben Hananiah to the royal palace and said to him, "Your God is likened unto a lion in your Scriptures. But it is known that a strong man can kill a lion. So how mighty can your God be?"

Rabbi Joshua responded that the Scriptures did not refer to an ordinary lion, but to a lion of the forest of Ilai. When the emperor said that he wanted to see the lion in question, the rabbi replied that this was not possible. The emperor stood his ground; otherwise, he threatened, Rabbi Joshua would be cut up into a thousand pieces.

Rabbi Joshua put on his phylacteries and prayer shawl and began to pray—and the lion of the forest of Ilai came out of its den. When the lion was 400 miles from the emperor's palace, he began to roar. Frightened by the terrible sound, all the pregnant women in Rome miscarried, and the walls of Rome crumbled. When the lion was 300 miles away, he roared again. All the teeth of the citizens of Rome fell out, and the emperor tumbled off his throne.

The emperor then hurried to the house of Rabbi Joshua and said, "I asked you to pray that I might see the lion of the forest of Ilai. Now I beg you to pray that I never see him. Make him return to his forest, for if he comes any closer he will destroy the entire world."

Once more Rabbi Joshua donned his phylacteries and prayer shawl and began to pray. The lion of the forest of Ilai returned to his lair—from whence, it is to be hoped, he will never emerge again.

אריה

THE STORK   The Hebrew word for "stork," *hasidah*, is derived from the term *hasid*, meaning "pious one." According to the Talmud, the bird received its name on account of its compassion and mercy. It brings food to its companions, and if the elder storks flag during migrations, the young ones carry them on their backs. Then why is the stork listed in the Bible among the unclean birds? A Hasidic saying supplies the answer—it is because the stork's compassion is reserved only for its own kind.

Distinguished for its keen sight, the stork can see any object in all of the Land of Israel from the vast distance of Babylon. Indeed, the stork looks ahead to the redemption of Israel from exile. The *Pirkei Shirah*, the compendium of hymns of praise for the Creator that all living things recite daily, asks: "What does the stork say?" It repeats the comforting prophecy of Isaiah: "Bid Jerusalem take heart, and proclaim unto her that her time of service is accomplished, that her guilt is paid off."

חסידה

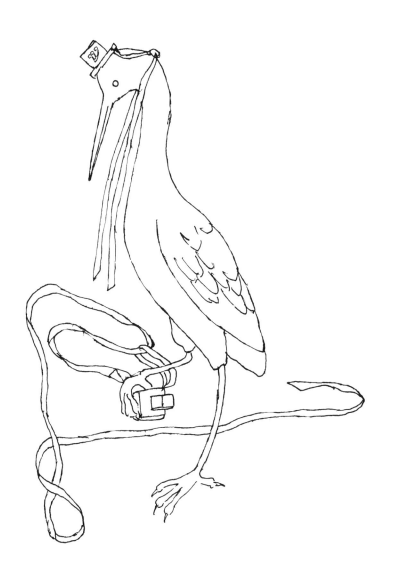

THE SNAIL "Let them [the wicked] . . . be like a snail that melts away as it moves." This denunciation from the Book of Psalms takes its imagery from the ancient belief that the moist streak left by a snail as it crawls along is subtracted from the substance of its body; the farther it creeps, the smaller it becomes, until it wastes away entirely.

A more benign association is with the aromatic spice *shehelet*, said to have been derived from the shell of a snail found in the Red Sea, which emits a pleasant odor when burned. *Shehelet* was one of the ingredients that, according to the Book of Exodus, composed the holy incense burned as an offering in the Tabernacle and later in the Temple. This fragrant offering is recalled in the ceremony of *Havdalah*, performed at the conclusion of the Sabbath and festivals, when blessings are recited over a cup of wine, a lit candle—and spices (placed in containers that have been fashioned from a variety of forms).

Certain mollusks have the ability to drill holes in rocks, dissolving the chalk and using it to form their shells. This may have inspired the legend of the *shamir*, the miraculous worm (possible cousin to the snail) that can cut through metals, precious stones, and even diamonds. Created, like the ram, on the twilight of the first Sabbath eve, the *shamir* is about the size of a grain of barley. It was kept wrapped in a woolen cloth inside a lead basket filled with barleycorn because no metal could contain it. It is said that the *shamir* was created for the sole purpose of splitting the stones used in the building of the Temple. (Tools made of iron were prohibited in the Temple construction, since iron is used in the forging of weapons of war.) When the Temple was destroyed, the *shamir* was lost. Only the Messiah knows its hiding place.

שבלול

THE OSTRICH   The ostrich, which has wings but is unable to fly, in its bodily structure and habits so resembles a camel that there are some who believe that it originated as a cross between a bird and a camel. Its ability to swallow any object is described in the Talmud in an account of an ostrich that devoured a pair of phylacteries. The Talmud also tells of an ostrich that swallowed gold pieces the size of an olive and ejected them fully polished. On account of its disproportionately small head the ostrich is considered a stupid bird. We read in the Book of Job: "God has deprived her [the ostrich] of wisdom, gave her no share of understanding, else she would soar on high, scoffing at the horse and the rider."

It was the custom to suspend the shell of an ostrich egg in every synagogue in Safed as well as over the tombs of the patriarchs in Hebron. Rabbi Jacob Emden, writing in the eighteenth century, explained the practice as follows: "The Jews . . . suspend ostrich eggs in their synagogues so as to intensify their devotion and to avoid being distracted. For the ostrich hatches its young by staring intently at the egg. This demonstrates how powerful sustained observation and concentration are. And indeed, they befit prayer."

בת יענה

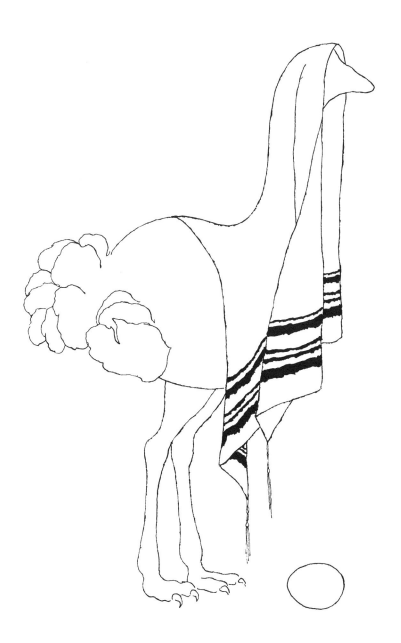

BEHEMOTH   Behemoth, the largest animal that lives on land, was fashioned from clay, so Jewish legend asserts, by the Holy One, blessed be He, on the sixth day of creation. It was created solely to be served at the end of days as one of the delicacies at the messianic banquet.

In the month of Tammuz, at the time of the summer solstice, when its strength is at its peak, behemoth rises on its hind legs and lets out a fearful echoing roar, so loud that all the animals in the world hear it. Terrified, the wild beasts become less ferocious and restrain themselves from preying on herds and flocks for the entire year.

According to the Book of Job, behemoth's "bones are like tubes of bronze, his limbs like iron rods. He is the first of God's works. Only his Maker can draw the sword against him." Each day behemoth gorges on fodder produced by a thousand mountains. The summer heat makes it so thirsty that all the water that flows through the bed of the Jordan during six months barely suffices for a single gulp. Therefore it was necessary to give it a water source entirely for its own use, a stream called Yubal that flows forth from Paradise into the wilderness of Dudain.

Because of its insatiable appetite, behemoth had to be prevented from multiplying, otherwise the world could not continue to exist. It is for this reason that God created only one such beast.

בהמות

THE GNAT   The rabbis tell us that many a species was created solely for the sake of a single member of its kind, to which some special historical mission was assigned. For example, the lowly gnat was called into being to cause the death of Titus, the Roman general who destroyed Jerusalem.

According to the Talmud, while Jerusalem was still in flames, Titus loaded the holy vessels of the destroyed Temple aboard a ship for transport to Rome so that he could parade the spoils of his victory. On the sea a violent gale sprang up, threatening to sink the ship. Titus cried out: "The God of the Jews may have dominion over the waters, but if He is really mighty let Him come up on dry land and fight with me." Whereupon a heavenly voice proclaimed: "Sinner and son of a sinner! There is a tiny creature in the world called a gnat. Go up on dry land and wage war with that!" The storm subsided, and the ship proceeded on its way.

When Titus landed at Ostia, a gnat flew into his nose and entered his brain. The insect remained inside Titus's head for seven years, buzzing incessantly. The suffering was intolerable. One day, as Titus was passing a blacksmith's shop, the gnat heard the clanging of the hammer and ceased its activity. Believing that a remedy had been found, Titus ordered a blacksmith to hammer before him each day. If the blacksmith was a non-Jew, he would be given four coins; if a Jew, he would be told that it was compensation enough to see the suffering of his enemy. However, the remedy worked for only thirty days because the gnat grew accustomed to the hammering and resumed its buzzing.

The gnat grew in size each day, feeding on Titus's brain until it finally caused his death. Physicians who opened his skull found a creature resembling a sparrow, weighing two pounds and with a beak made of brass and claws of iron.

Titus's remains were cremated. In accordance with his dying command, his ashes were carried to distant places and scattered over the seven seas so that the God of the Jews would not be able to find him and bring him to trial for the destruction of the Temple.

יתוש

THE SALAMANDER   The salamander, according to Jewish folklore, is a creature fashioned from a fire that burns seven days and seven nights. The medieval commentator Rashi contended that the fire must burn for seven years. The salamander's miraculous property is its ability to offer natural protection against fire. For it is said that a salamander can extinguish a flame merely by passing through it; a fire so quenched is impossible to rekindle. If one smears a hand or any other part of the body with the blood of a salamander, that part is safeguarded against fire.

The wicked people who lived at the time of the Great Flood boasted that if the world were to be destroyed by fire, the punishment of Gehinnom (Hell), they would save themselves with the blood of a salamander. But God destroyed the world by water, with rain falling from above, and scalding waters, hot as fire, gushing up from below.

When King Ahaz, who is counted among the worst of sinners, was about to sacrifice his son Hezekiah to the fires of the idol Moloch, the child's mother painted her son with the blood of the salamander. As a result, the flames did not harm him. Hezekiah grew up to be king and to be numbered among the most pious of Israel.

סלמנדרא

LEVIATHAN   Leviathan, vividly described in the Book of Job, rules over all the creatures of the sea. ("His bared teeth strike terror. His protective scales are his pride. . . . He makes the depths seethe like a cauldron; he makes the sea boil like an ointment-pot.") For three hours each day, according to Rabbi Judah, the Holy One, blessed be He, sports with this spectacular creature.

The enormousness of Leviathan is attested to in the Talmud by Rabbi Johanan: "Once we went in a ship and saw a fish which put his head out of the water. He had horns upon which was written: 'I am three hundred miles in length, and yet enter this day into the jaws of Leviathan.' "

Legend has it that originally two leviathans were created, but when it seemed as if the pair might annihilate the world with their combined strength, God destroyed one. It is said that the fins of Leviathan radiate a brilliant light and that its eyes, in the words of Job, "are like the glimmerings of dawn," illuminating the oceans. The "garments of skin" fashioned by God for Adam and Eve, also known as "garments of light," were made from the skin of the slain leviathan.

In the *Apocalypse of Abraham* it is written that the entire world, as well as the great sea that encompasses it, rests on four pillars and that these pillars rest on one of the fins of Leviathan. It is also written that Leviathan lies on the primordial abyss, which otherwise would flood the earth.

Like the ziz and behemoth, Leviathan is destined to be the food of the pious in the world to come. And its skin is to be stretched as a canopy from the walls of Jerusalem to illuminate the world.

לויתן

THE RAVEN   One year after the rains of the Great Flood had subsided, Noah asked the raven to go forth from the ark and to return with a report on the condition of the waters. The raven refused and hid under the wings of an eagle. When Noah found him, the raven pleaded that another bird be given the assignment. Not content to let the matter rest, the raven then accused Noah of coveting the raven's mate for himself; this, he allowed, was the reason why Noah chose him for a mission that was certain to end in death. An enraged Noah cried out: "May God curse the mouth which has spoken such evil against me!" All the animals in the ark said, "Amen!"—and the raven's heretofore dulcet voice became the harsh caw that we hear to this day.

Similarly, the raven had only himself to blame for his awkward hop. Envious of the graceful walk of the dove, the raven tried to copy it. Instead, he broke all his bones. When he tried to resume his original gait, he could no longer remember it. Of the raven the proverb says: "He who seeks more than he has will be left with less."

As it happened, the raven finally did leave the ark, but he never returned. As the waters receded, he remained behind to feed on the carnage left by the Flood. As punishment, the raven's feathers, which originally were pure white, turned pitch black.

עורב

THE ASS   A useful domesticated beast—created for the purpose of "carrying burdens," as the Talmud notes—the ass is also regarded as the most stupid of creatures. Because of this, it is the frequent subject of popular proverbs ("The donkey freezes even in the summer month of Tammuz"). To be called an ass is considered a great insult.

Undoubtedly, the most famous ass is the biblical mount that carried the sorcerer Balaam. Balaam was summoned by Balak, king of Moab, to ride forth into the desert and curse the Israelites, whose victories en route to the Promised Land were proving alarming. Balaam's pronouncements were considered especially potent, for as Balak said to him: "I know that he whom you bless is blessed indeed, and he whom you curse is cursed." On the way to his malevolent mission, Balaam was confronted by an angel with a sword in his hand. Only the ass saw the angel, and three times it swerved from the road, refusing to continue even though Balaam beat it. The ass was then granted the power of speech and reproached Balaam for the ill treatment. "Then the Lord uncovered Balaam's eyes," and he too saw the angel. And instead of a curse, he pronounced blessing upon Israel.

Balaam's ass, according to tradition, was another of the special creatures created at the close of the sixth day of Creation at dusk. It was said to have been the dam of the ass ridden by Abraham when he traveled to the sacrifice of Isaac and was declared to be the same ass that later bore Moses' wife and her sons in Egypt. One day, this very same ass will also serve the Messiah, who according to the prophet Zechariah is to come "riding on an ass."

אתון

THE SPIDER   The spider, like the ant, is honored in the Book of Proverbs as one of the minuscule creatures that are "the wisest of the wise." As it is written, "You can catch the spider in your hands, yet it is found in royal palaces."

Legend tells us that when David was a young shepherd, he observed a spider spinning its web. He thought to himself: "What is the purpose of such a creature? It spends its lifetime spinning, but its webs can never make a garment. All of its undertakings are filled with vain hopes." Whereupon a voice from Heaven called out: "David! You mock the Lord's creatures now, but a time will come when you will see why it [the spider] was created."

Several years passed and the shepherd boy, after slaying the giant Goliath with a slingshot, became the hero of the people and the favorite of King Saul. But as David's popularity grew, so did the king's jealousy, and in his fury Saul imagined that David was plotting to seize the throne. When David learned of Saul's intention to kill him, he fled the palace and sought refuge in the wilderness.

Once, while David was hiding in a cave, he heard Saul and a troop of soldiers approaching. They were about to enter the cave in search of their quarry when the Holy One, blessed be He, sent a spider to weave a web across the entrance. When Saul saw the web, he told his men to look elsewhere, reasoning that David could not be in the cave, else he would have broken the web.

After Saul and his soldiers departed, David came out of the cave and kissed the spider that had saved him. He then took up his harp and composed a psalm of praise to the Lord.

עכביש

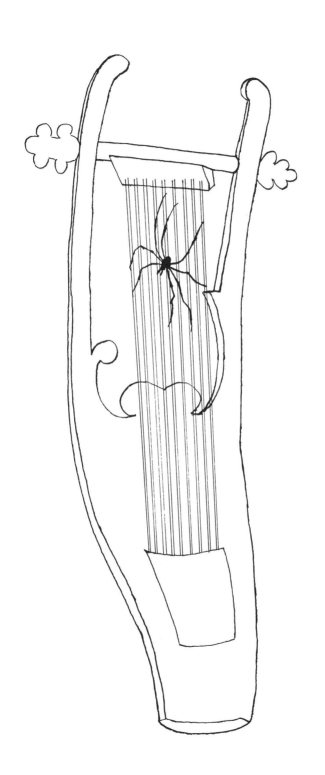

THE FOX   In the Talmud the treacherous fox is often contrasted with the kingly lion: "Be rather the tail among lions than the head of foxes." In the Book of Ezekiel false prophets are compared with foxes. The tail of a fox suspended between the eyes of a horse gave the equine protection from the evil eye. A fox's tooth was carried either to promote or to prevent sleep, depending on whether the tooth was taken from a live fox or a dead one.

The fox is perhaps the favorite animal of Jewish folklore. Rabbi Meir is said to have compiled three hundred fox fables, but only three survived three generations after the sage's death. There are numerous tales regarding the fox's unscrupulous nature, many concerning its inordinate appetite. For instance, a fox overeats in an orchard and grows so large that it is forced to fast in order to get out again. A fox tries to convince a bird of a new law forbidding birds to sit on trees so that the fox may enjoy the exclusive benefit of the fruit. A fox sits as a mediator between two animals quarreling over a piece of cheese and eats it all.

In many tales the cunning fox manages to outsmart the larger and wilder animals, once outwitting even the Angel of Death. A fox persuades a wolf to visit the local bazaar, a place stocked with food, by claiming to be in possession of an "entrance certificate." When the wolf is beaten up by the townspeople, the brazen fox tells the unfortunate wolf that the inhabitants are illiterate and cannot read the certificate. The wolf is killed, and the fox eats its carcass. In another tale a fox plays sick and tells a lion that the cure the physicians have prescribed is binding. The lion ties the fox up, the fox declares his pain gone, and the lion frees him. Later, when the lion is taken sick, he asks the fox to tie *him* up. The fox obliges, stones the lion's head, kills him, and, of course, eats him.

שועל

THE COCK   The Talmud bids us to pronounce the following blessing upon hearing the cock crow each morning: "Praised be Thou, O God, Lord of the world, that gavest understanding to the cock to distinguish between day and night." According to the Zohar, when God visits Paradise each midnight to confer with the souls of the pious, all the trees break out in adoration and their song awakens the cock, which in turn begins to praise God, at the same time calling upon men to praise the Lord.

The crowing of the cock drives away the demons, and the image of a cock on amulets is a potent device against the evil eye. According to Rabbi Judah the Pious, a cock that upsets a vessel should be killed immediately because evil spirits have seized it. To produce rain, one must kill a white cock, tear it apart, and extract its entrails, filling them with white pepper, honey, milk, myrhh, frankincense, crocus, and old wine and holding them up to the sun, all the while reciting an incantation.

A Hebrew synonym for "rooster" is *gever*, meaning "man." This relates to the custom of *kapparot* (atonement), performed on the eve of the Day of Atonement. To carry out the ritual, one swings a fowl (a cock for a male, a hen for a female) over the head while praying that the fowl, when slaughtered, serve as a substitute for the individual: "This cock (hen) goes to its death that I may enter into a long and happy life and into peace."

תרנגול

THE SWINE   According to the Talmud, "ten measures
of diseases descended into the world, of which the swine
took nine." The many maladies from which the pig suffers
are said to stem from its disgusting habits of eating everything and finding its food everywhere. The rabbis held the
creature in such abhorrence that the Talmud endeavors to
avoid even mentioning it by name, often referring to the pig
as *davar aher*, "another thing."

The boar, called "the swine of the woods" in the Book of
Psalms, is described as a beast that crushes its prey, eats
its fill, and tramples the rest of the carcass. Fittingly, the
boar served as the symbol of the Roman Tenth Legion,
whose soldiers set Jerusalem aflame and destroyed the Second Temple, encamping on its ashes. Under Roman rule,
Jewish tradition records, the people of Israel suffered such
agony that they could not wipe away all their tears. The
tears that remained were etched into their cheeks and left
permanent scars.

In ancient Jewish writings, the swine thus became symbolic of Rome; both displayed the same deceitful charac-
teristics. The Midrash asks: "Why is Rome compared with
a swine?" The swine, the sages note, is ritually unclean and
may not be eaten because, although it has cloven hooves,
it does not chew its cud. When the swine is lying down it
puts out its hooves as if to deceive those looking upon it into
thinking it is a permitted (kosher) animal.

For Jews, Rome remains the byword for perfidy. The
swine, most despised of beasts, shares this ignominy.

חזיר

THE AZAZEL-GOAT   In accordance with the biblical injunction, every year on the Day of Atonement, two male goats, selected as if twins, would be brought to the Temple in Jerusalem for the special ministrations of the High Priest. The fate of each would be decided by the casting of lots. On one lot would be written, "For the Lord"; on the other, "For Azazel." The goat chosen for the Lord would be slaughtered as a sin-offering. The Azazel-goat would have a crimson thread twisted around its horns, and the High Priest would press his hands upon the head of the goat, confessing over it the inquities of the people. Laden with the sins of Israel, the goat would be led into the wilderness.

Azazel? Some say it was a steep cliff from which the goat would be hurled, a cliff so high and rugged that before the goat fell halfway it would be smashed to pieces. Others suggest that Azazel was a goat-demon who haunted the desert and required appeasement. In yet another version of the story, Azazel is Satan himself, and the goat is a propitiation to forestall the Evil One's interference with the atonement of sins on the holiest of days.

The Talmud recounts that when the scapegoat reached Azazel, a thread of crimson wool tied to the Temple entrance would turn white, a sign that the sins of the people had been forgiven (reminiscent of the verse in Isaiah: "Be your sins like crimson, they can turn snow-white"). During the forty years preceding the destruction of the Second Temple, the thread remained crimson. It was said that the Temple was destroyed because so great were the sins of Israel that all the letters of the Torah had been transgressed.

שעיר לעזאזל

THE GOLDEN CALF   Before ascending Mount Sinai to receive the Torah, Moses informed the Israelites that he would return after forty days. When the people saw that he delayed in coming down, they grew apprehensive. A legend relates that Satan caused the Israelites to see a bier passing across the skies on which lay a figure resembling Moses, thus confirming their fear that Moses had died. Thereupon the Israelites demanded that Aaron make them a god, one like the Egyptians', before which they could dance and which would guide them on their journey through the desert.

Threatened with death if he failed to comply, Aaron instructed the men to bring him their wives' jewelry, anticipating that the women would refuse. This indeed proved the case, but the men then donated their own ornaments, which Aaron then threw into a fire. Out of the flames there emerged a molten golden calf, which skipped about as if it were a living being. The people danced around it in worship. According to Rabbi Judah, Satan himself had entered into the calf to lead Israel astray.

When Moses returned from the mountain, he saw the calf and the dancing, and in his great anger smashed the Tablets of the Law. He burned the calf, ground it to powder, and scattered the dust upon the water, making the people drink from it. Everyone who had kissed the calf immediately turned to gold. The supremacy over the Angel of Death that the Jews had achieved for accepting the Torah was taken away. And, it is said, there is not a sorrow that Israel has suffered that is not in great part retribution for the sin of worshipping the golden calf.

עגל הזהב

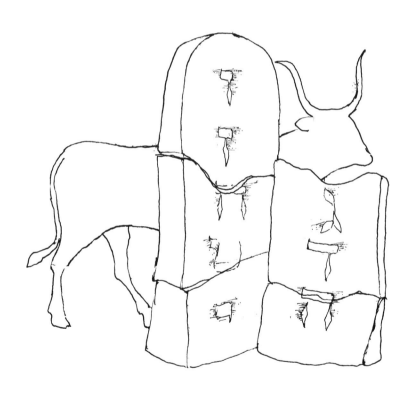

THE DOVE   The sages ask, why is Israel compared with a dove? It is because the dove, meekest and gentlest of all the birds, is also the most persecuted. Unable to fight with its beak or claws, it has only its wings to protect itself. A pursued dove never ceases its flight; when one wing is fatigued, it continues on with the other. So it is with the people of Israel. Though persecuted and deprived of half its strength, Israel cannot be completely destroyed, but continues to live.

The Throne of Solomon was second only to the Temple in its splendor. At the throne's summit there reposed a dove with its claws set on a hawk, symbolizing that a time would come when all the enemies of Israel would be delivered into the dove's—Israel's—hands.

Each year on the eve of Tisha B'Av (the fast day marking the destruction of the Temple), a white dove resting in a recess of the Western Wall joins the people of Israel in their mourning. The sound of its weeping cleaves the heavens all night and all the next day until sunset. For all the other days of the year the dove remains silent.

In contrast with the raven, symbol of evil and egotism (the first creature to leave the ark, but not to return), the dove epitomizes fidelity. Sent forth from the ark by Noah, the dove returned with an olive branch in its bill. Some say that the dove found the branch on a tree on the Mount of Olives, indicating that the Flood did not reach the Holy Land. Others say that even the Holy Land was flooded and that the olive branch came from Paradise, whose gates opened to receive the dove.

יונה

THE GREAT FISH   The great fish associated with
Jonah, like certain other creatures we have noted, was created to fulfill a special destiny—in this instance, to harbor
Jonah in his distress at sea. When the great fish swallowed
the prophet, the Zohar says, Jonah actually died of fright
but was brought back to life. The fish was also said to have
perished, but three days later it was restored to life and returned Jonah to shore.

A further legend relates that when Jonah entered its
belly, the fish explained that its charge had been fulfilled
and that it must therefore present itself before the sea
dragon Leviathan to be consumed. But when Jonah saw
Leviathan he exclaimed, "I have been brought here to know
your hiding place, for I am to slaughter you in the world to
come and serve you for a meal to the pious of this earth."
Observing the sign of the covenant on Jonah's flesh, the
frightened sea dragon swam away. Jonah and the great fish
were both saved.

The grateful fish then revealed to Jonah all the mysteri-
ous and wondrous places of the sea. The prophet was taken
to see the river from which all oceans flow and to the place
where the Children of Israel crossed the Red Sea. The eyes
of the fish served Jonah as windows; suspended in the fish's
entrails was a pearl that shone brightly, enabling Jonah to
see all the things in the sea down to the very bottom.

Jonah remained inside the belly of the great fish for three
days and three nights. When Jonah was shown the Foundation Stone set in the abyss below the Temple, he im-
plored God's forgiveness and pleaded that he be allowed to
go on to Nineveh to preach to its people about their wicked
ways. Since all prayers offered up from beneath the Temple
of the Lord are answered, the great fish spewed the prophet
out upon dry land. He proceeded at once to Nineveh to
carry out the mission the Lord had commanded him.

These miracles were all witnessed by the sailors who had
cast Jonah into the sea. In awe of what they had seen, they
tossed their idols into the waters and sailed back to Jaffa.
They then went up to Jerusalem to be circumcised and to
live out their days as pious converts.

דג גדול

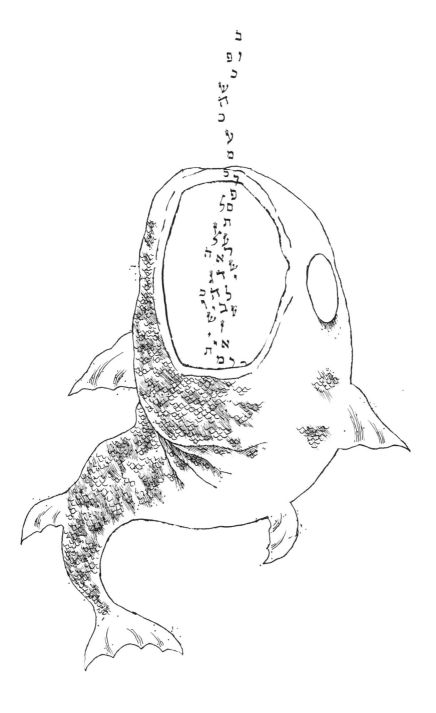

THE UNICORN   The animal in the Bible that is called *tahash* (variously translated as "seal," "badger," or "dolphin"), whose hide was used to cover the Tabernacle, in Jewish legend has come to be identified with the unicorn.

According to the Talmud, the unicorn was the first animal offered by Adam as a sacrifice to the Lord. At the conclusion of the first Sabbath, Adam and Eve observed the setting of the sun for the first time. Seized with fear, they wept the entire night, believing that their sin had caused the world to end. When the sun rose the next morning, however, they realized that what they had witnessed was the natural order of events. Adam then brought a unicorn as an offering to the Lord. The site of the sacrifice, it is said, was Mount Moriah, where Abraham would later bind Isaac and where in due course the Temple was to stand.

The unicorn is described as the fiercest of animals. One thrust of its horn could kill an elephant, and even a lion would flee before it. When Moses recited the blessings of the twelve tribes of Israel before his death, he blessed Manasseh (one of the two branches of Joseph) as follows: "As the unicorn with his horn pushes away all other animals, so too shall Joseph's sons rule the nations, even to the end of the earth." The symbol of the tribe of Manasseh is the unicorn.

Controversy has centered on the unusual head of the *tahash*. Some authorities maintained that although the one-horned creature existed in the time of Moses, it has long since vanished. The scholars also debated as to whether the *tahash* belonged to the class of *behemah* (domestic animals) or of *hayah* (beasts). In any event, once the construction of the Tabernacle was completed, the creature disappeared so that, as Rabbi Johanan taught, its skin could be used as clothing for the righteous in the world to come.

תחש

NEBUCHADNEZZAR AS A BEAST Nebuchadnezzar, the king of Babylon who destroyed Jerusalem and the Temple of Solomon, so terrorized the people that during his lifetime no one dared to laugh. His favorite pet was said to be a lion with a snake coiled around its neck, and he was reputed to dine on live animals, particularly rabbits.

Under his orders, the Jews exiled to Babylon were not permitted to rest for even a moment lest they use the opportunity to pray to God for mercy. On their way into exile, the princes of Judah were put in chains. When Nebuchadnezzar saw that they carried no loads, he ordered that Torah scrolls be torn up into pieces and made into sacks, which were filled with sand. The sacks were loaded on the backs of the princes being borne off to Babylon. At the sight of this humiliation, all of Israel wept.

In his ultimate arrogance, Nebuchadnezzar declared himself a god, and for that he was punished as none before him. The Holy One, blessed be He, changed him into a beast; the lower part of his body resembled a lion, and like an ox he foraged for grass. In this animal form he went on the rampage. At the end of forty days, his reason returned, as did his human shape, and for the next forty days he bitterly lamented his sins. Then God took mercy on him, and the seven years of punishment that had been decreed against him were reduced to seven months. After his return to the throne, Nebuchdnezzar did penance for the rest of his days and subsisted solely on vegetables.

נבוכדנאצר

THE BARNACLE GOOSE A curious notion prevailed in the Middle Ages that this bird—a European goose that breeds in the far north and is related to, but larger than, the brant—was generated from the barnacle, a shellfish growing on a flexible stem and adhering to loose timber and the bottoms of ships. The fable was echoed in Jewish sources, in which the fowl in question were said to grow on trees near the sea, hanging by their beaks until they fell off. Reference to the legend is found in the Zohar, which says that Rabbi Aba saw a tree from whose branches geese grew.

Medieval Jewish scholars in France and Germany debated as to whether the barnacle goose, given its origin, was to be considered a bird, a plant, or even a fish. The anonymous compiler of the legal compendium *Kol Bo*, citing various authorities, concludes that it is a bird, but an unclean one and hence forbidden as food. On the other hand, Rabbenu Tam, grandson of Rashi, allowed it to be eaten, as did Rabbi Samuel Ha-Hasid of Speier and his son, Rabbi Judah Ha-Hasid of Regensburg (provided that, in common with other species of permitted fowl, it was slaughtered after the Jewish fashion).

Of course, one first has to find the tree that bears the barnacle goose.

ברנטיאוש

THE ZIZ   The fabulous ziz, whose single scriptural mention (in the Book of Psalms) gave rise to rich imaginings, is a bird monstrous in size, ruling over all the other birds. Its wings are reputed to be so enormous that when they unfurl day turns into night. These pinions protect the earth from the storms that blow from the south.

If the Holy One, blessed be He, had not in His infinite mercy created the ziz to provide protection for the weak and defenseless among the avian creatures, they would have been destroyed long ago by their more ferocious fellows. Every year, on the first day of the month of Tishri, the ziz lets out a horrible shriek while flapping its wings. The falcons, the vultures, and the other birds of prey tremble and restrain their appetites.

The Talmud records a "sighting" of the ziz. It once happened that travelers on a ship noticed a bird standing in the water. The waves covered merely its feet, and its head knocked against the sky. The onlookers thought the water couldn't be very deep at that point, and they decided to bathe there. A heavenly voice warned them, "Alight not here! Once a carpenter's axe slipped from his hand at this spot, and it took seven years to touch bottom." The bird the travelers saw was none other than the ziz.

The name *ziz* is derived from the varied tastes the bird's flesh is said to have: it tastes like "this" and it tastes like "that," in Hebrew, *zeh va-zeh*. Even though it is well known that when the Messiah comes, a new Torah will be given which will dispense with the current dietary regulations, the ziz is already considered kosher.

The ziz is one of the three delicacies—the others are behemoth and Leviathan—destined to delight the palates of the righteous in the world to come. Tradition holds that Moses himself will serve the ziz at the messianic banquet.

Once, it was reported, a ziz's egg accidentally fell to earth and shattered. The fluid flooded sixty cities, and the shock crushed three hundred giant cedars in the forests of Lebanon. Fortunately, such accidents do not happen frequently.

SELECTED BIBLIOGRAPHY

Bickerman, Elias. *Four Strange Books of the Bible*. New York, Schocken, 1967.

Encyclopedia Judaica. 16 vols. Jerusalem, Keter Publishing House, 1971–72.

The Fathers According to Rabbi Nathan. Translated by Judah Goldin. New Haven, Yale University Press, 1955.

Feliks, J. *Animal World of the Bible*. Tel Aviv, Sinai, 1962.

Ginzberg, Louis. *Legends of the Jews*. 7 vols. Philadelphia, The Jewish Publication Society of America, 1909–46.

The Jewish Encyclopedia. 12 vols. New York, Funk and Wagnalls Co., 1901–1906.

Ma'aseh Book. Translated by Moses Gaster. Philadelphia, The Jewish Publication Society of America, 1981.

Midrash Rabbah. 5 vols. Translated by H. Freedman and Maurice Simon. London, Soncino, 1939.

Nadich, Judah. *Jewish Legends of the Second Commonwealth*. Philadelphia, The Jewish Publication Society of America, 1983.

Noy, Dov. *The Jewish Animal Tale*. Haifa, Haifa Municipality Ethnological Museum, Folklore Archives, 1976.

Pirke de-Rabbi Eliezer. Translated by Gerald Friedlander. New York, Sepher-Hermon Press, 1965.

Raphael, Chaim. *The Walls of Jerusalem*. New York, Alfred A. Knopf, 1968.

Trachtenberg, Joshua. *Jewish Magic and Superstition*. New York, Behrman House, 1939.

Vilnay, Zev. *Legends of Galilee, Jordan, and Sinai*. Philadelphia, The Jewish Publication Society of America, 1978.

———. *Legends of Jerusalem*. Philadelphia, The Jewish Publication Society of America, 1973.

The Zohar. 5 vols. Translated by Maurice Simon and Harry Sperling. London, Soncino, 1934.

The rendition of biblical verses in this text generally follows the new Jewish Publication Society translation of the Scriptures (*The Torah*, 1962; *The Prophets*, 1978; *The Writings*, 1982).